MILLION POEMS JOURNAL

Jordan Davis

*For Bill Austin
before the hurricane
with gratitude*

9/16/03

Jordan Davis

FAUX PRESS

CAMBRIDGE, MA

Copyright © 2003 by Jordan Davis
All rights reserved.

Some of these poems appeared previously in the following publications:
Verse, Combo, Quid, East Village Poetry Web, Long Shot, Kiosk,
Washington Review, Faucheuse, Lungfull!, Nine-Zero,
Poetry New York, and Hanging Loose.

The author would like to thank the Fund for Poetry
for its generous assistance.

Faux Press books are edited by Jack Kimball
Cover design by George Schneeman
Book design by *typeslowly*

Distributed to the trade through
SPD: Small Press Distribution
www.spdbooks.org

ISBN 0-9710371-8-3

07 06 05 04 03   98765432 FIRST PRINTING
Faux Press
www.fauxpress.com

CONTENTS

- 9 — ANYTHING SUDDENLY
- 10 — THE TOURIST AND THE TSARIST
- 12 — POETRY AND CAPITAL
- 14 — *How sexy it is*
- 15 — A FANCY BEAR
- 17 — *I am not quite an old Frenchie*
- 18 — NATIONALISM
- 19 — SEXISM
- 20 — POETRY IN MOTION
- 21 — PLAYING THE STANDARDS
- 22 — FALSE FRIENDS
- 23 — *Now that her book was out*
- 24 — *They're binding the hills*
- 25 — *I miss your pussy*
- 26 — LIGHTNING IN MONTANA
- 27 — FORBIDDEN IRONING
- 28 — FOR A MOMENT'S CREOLE
- 29 — JUBILEE OF EVENING
- 30 — EASE OF PLAIN
- 31 — DEEP CHERRY
- 32 — TALKING TO ANYTHING
- 33 — TEA SLACKS
- 34 — THE TRUE STORY OF THE APARTMENT
- 36 — BOOKS AND THINGS
- 37 — FORCE OF LOCAL PERMISSION
- 38 — MEERKAT
- 39 — POEM
- 40 — TOAST
- 43 — LET'S FLOAT
- 44 — TELEKINESIS
- 45 — MILLION POEMS JOURNAL
- 49 — READY DESIRE
- 50 — COPPER BEECH

51	LAND CAMERA
52	HAIKU
53	SOME EFFECTS OF THE BOOK
54	NOTEBOOK AND CHOIR
55	REGULAR DIAMONDS
56	SOMEONE ON THE CARPET
57	POEM MIDDLE OF THE NIGHT
58	SONNET
59	ARE YOU TO BE MY NAMIBIA?
60	ROTTEN FLOOR
61	THE PARADE OF THE NOTEBOOKS
66	WOMAN (A.S)
69	THOSE KEROUACS MAY YET BE SUNS RA
70	EPISTEMOLOGY WANTS YOU
74	O BOTH
75	TO THE ZEE AND BACK
81	*In the evening the air time*
82	EXPLODED VIEW
84	LAST MUCHAS GRACIAS
88	NASHVILLE

for KENNETH KOCH

ANYTHING SUDDENLY

Do you have in the feminism of your immediacy
Enough wine for the two hundred readers of secrets?
Or is the serenade contour of the breeze enough
To get them speaking sparks, red books stacked
On white shelves being tipped into the fire,
Goddamn happy to letter perspective again
And grandeur again and fireflies seen through
Window fans are the ocean, yikes I'm white!
Disturbed and amused by gold lipstick on someone
Scuffling in my longing, sure, anything suddenly

THE TOURIST AND THE TSARIST

Sunday morning
I get up early
For New York
In the middle of spring
Put on my blank pants
Her idea
To go for a walk
And a swim
And then to the library
To study for her exam
A year's latin
Balancing on the curb

Down eight avenues
Burning with a magnifying glass
Past babies on their knees
Down tree streets
All delivery entrances
Squatter churches
The plane tree
Walls fading coca-cola smoke
Mattresses, the buckling brick
A desk rolls down the street on its back

Dresses hang in the window
Against the glass
The dollar specials stars on the building
Shade falls down comic book tops
Of the fence
Orange cough-drop hydrant bazaars
Deplete turntable blazers' crossword trust

Even dumpsters shine beer for
A bird at war
With a bottlecap in the marigolds

Oh sweet reaching to stem
Gauzy lumber west up the pinwheels
Once you're dead
You're flown out
On a smoking
Passenger capacity
Jerome

Latin or no
Something else parks the car
Meet me in the bookstore
In gold and silver
Black and white and red
Silk panties

However
Curl of violin
Is this woman complete
As people are
Chances for happiness?
Am I?

POETRY AND CAPITAL

                lights on! and chocolate milk
Defends the late triage of our distortions, kingdom
Bought with phlox. Oh stereo, retroverted girl
Only you understand the exchange rates of words ailing like
Chimney that has been shat down by pogroms of vinca,
The minstrels apoplectic with receipts,
Garlanding their Isis with poppies
As the sweet neologisms arrive from their apartments
Creaming on the sinning flourishes. Credit! I appeal
To your franking condoms of a certainty,
Will you ululate along these tumid friezes?
For canticles and previous shears you
Have reboomed and broached, peevish indeed,
But ghastly to the kinks of radio windowsill fame,
I'd rather not drink against the side of the building
With rehearsal and demonstrate my vacant treeline with cark
Maybe raining on dangerous evening cicadas
As it did one night, Genji admiring the tits
Of a merman debating policy in the fo'c'sle with an albatross
Which as you may know is the prim sycophant of
Our poltroon, always slavishly modulating the ancient vases
Into decanters of high-test gin, ah, that Jehovah!
Sugar Ray something, as they doubted first this musk-ox
Then that doormaid's torso. Patrician frappes passed
Such as "Why don't you will her to make me an omelette?"
For three-thousand-six-hundred-fifty days, to be
Unwilling to breathe, this asiatic rubble on the bloodline
Bumpershoots, deflating what elegiasts
Perpetuate with weathered numberings of health
And wattage, if not through sheer sex in brine,
Always an adagio in camphor plague-rat candor,

Marrying the wrong-way gymnast, the violet rose,
It's all love when a surface fails
And that beast the beloved looks, leans over,
And pulls you out like a bell. All that sloping
Misty snowbrink fidgets the lake-blank singer
Into hardcore gillyflower vedantisms, travel without
Husband or daughters, foliage relenting on the fringe,
Feeling like a scottish cookie in a Pennsylvania depot.
I won't decorate the quasars of well-meaning
Except as the carriage rises with the city lights
From gold to gold and back

How sexy it is
To hear an edge
Of plastic being scratched
And then the whole thing torn
Off behind you when you know that
A sexy girl is sitting behind you
On the inbound LIRR car 2977
The door ajar then wide open

A FANCY BEAR

> *"what will fancy bear"*—Sir Philip Sidney

Come on over.
We have a video
Of a bear
Knocking down a house.
Bring beer. Cruelty has no part in love
Don't stand there like a rosebush
Why will no one say the truth
About what they think and love?
What does this question say
About me? Letters fall
Like a black dress
Singing of the body
Of a serious woman
Is that the truth?
I couldn't hear what she said she had taken.
A fastener? A vasty black time?
Peacock feathers, composition seas,
The sweat of gold,
Is 'distilleries blown down' what I think of you?
The convertible won't stop
The highway converging
Its green stings out of reach
A wide net takes you
For the present of green
Mallows from the cemetery
Green roads I feel your lateral secrets
As something excellent
Plays a game

Sorry and sorries to the cool
Unattended white ruins

To be struggled up night
Why do I always rehearse my real love
How shaking is forgotten
And the body is
A weed
Severe. Angels have grabbed the four corners
Of paradise
And hauled it away
In a red and blue cloud,
And at the phone on the spot
Is posted a silent light. White spirals
Of sunny morning obscure it,
The tiny halo of a knot
Goes on out of the city.
Divide it in three like a painting,
Giraffes in the sea yes
Well or anyway the waves
Languor that makes
Your brother and sister
And present you with a handbook

Elsewhere is being held
Tenderly! Truly! Here there
Are floods fireworks and
The mania the still hours of hot
And quiet reading oh do
You think so? Accustomed
To the blush of
Pages bent toward
Placid and damp streetlight,
The bass
Cuts into the bone
Around the heart. O but is it
Temporary? We just got here.

I am not quite an old Frenchie
Like Jean-Baptiste Couture
My great-great-grandfather
Who edited Le Messenger
The French-Canadian newspaper
Of Lewiston, Maine
For fifty years
And who for his fights
With the Catholic Church
Of Maine received
An interdiction—
Not quite an excommunication—

NATIONALISM

The German part of me drinks beer
And stares into the sun
The Welsh, Scots, Irish parts of me
Take whiskey "from the gun"
The English part prefers caffeine
But also treasures rum
But give wine to the French of me
And then your night's begun—

Poetry, opinions, brutality and charm,
The blue ink of the south seas
On the brim of your attorney's cap
Parade! the silent heroes from their graves
Climb out ravenous for love.
Stone-eyes, drink some water and guard
The raw gentility there, the better decorum:
Raucous, undisgraced, exemplifying
A generosity to accident.

SEXISM

My lips are chapped
And the world is full of girls!
Three three oh six a woman shouts
Standing on a street corner. A woman coming
Around the corner steps or tries to behind
Me as I try to do the same for her. We laugh.
What did you say the number was shouts
A woman on the other corner.

POETRY IN MOTION

What does that mean
Success in verse? I think
It can't be skee
Ball at the beach
And the hose of clover
To be traffic as
Lost from the thought
As the ghost on the stairs
Singing tall and smiling
In the singular environment
Of a penny dripping
On the tracks hands
Behind your back the white
Light elbow underneath
Revenue as bulldog is
To take the chain
From under the shirt
And two days go by
Falsetto in the heartbreak
Of red girders as girls
On the other side open
Their mail and go glad
Like a ramp soap
Gushes down at
Midnight

PLAYING THE STANDARDS

What happens in the coffeeshops
Is not your business. Esteem
Your fastidi grassi champagne filth.
The organ is playing "smuk" angels
For the king to be born,
And our house has a balcony too.
Come in the ambulance with me
And let me lift your skirt, you
Dazzling unknown form!

FALSE FRIENDS

They were driving their friend's dog
South to be in a movie.
Formerly they had great hopes
For him—now for his dog.

Estranged from his father
He would catch himself
Burning hot in the bathroom mirror
Making the call of a warbler.

Now that her book was out
And her husband was no longer
Competitive on the golf circuit
She was happy to keep the secret
Of her name. They would play
Tennis and be admired for her
Looks and backhand as much as
His masters and opens. She was
Striking in a pony tail and
Her verse was clean and strong.
She wrote about people in Maine
And Massachusetts towns and only
In an occasional analogy to
Sidelines did she hint of her
Relation. He loved her. He
Flipped through Trollope and Clancy
Novels at night as she sat
In front of her three-line screen
Adding lines and taking lines away.

Their daughter was drunk off her ass
At a boarding school in Delaware.

They're binding the hills
To score them with the time
Seedlings in June
And the houses which are the perfection
Beings mar a little substation
How pleasant their voices are
When you don't know what they're
Of sticking around in the middle class
Tree swept back and sunglasses
Are your reward
Flashing yellow lights
Saying two rows ahead
Silver dollar shows

I miss your pussy
You're the only one who likes my jokes
And I miss your ass and hips your clever

Getting up on your elbows to look
I miss sucking on your rose sour tits
Your frantic hard kisses

And how you said "just a taste."
But was I ever so awful as when I was with you?
D) Not enough information provided.

Anyway, I hope there's something pleasant to remember
For you, about me,
From those year-like hours.

2.

(I miss but was I aiming?
You catch me anyway)

LIGHTNING IN MONTANA

I felt my head
Pushed between my shoulder

Blades and a pincushion in
Me pushed out as if I'd

Walked into a cotton ball
It was soft when I landed

Fifty feet away over a six
Foot redwood fence

FORBIDDEN IRONING

Antifreeze butterfly cathode,
I dare you, trumpet bigwheel.

The rain is a permit for
Sudden isostasy dreams,

Home is a list of forbidden
Din. Egret fanfare greenhouse,

I dare you, oboe ironing hill.
Tomorrow you will be read.

A man is a game floods are
The roads and who am I who

Is hummingbird jape knocker?
Is Africa England in a jar?

Lovelife manservant nobodies,
If the water rises to roses

(Accident in the passing lane,
Orotund Princess, Queen Round

Spinning on the log thieves
Sun), then under a visor warden

Wakes us from our songs. I too
Sing your zoo across puddles.

FOR A MOMENT'S CREOLE

I'll give a basketball
To the Statue of Liberty
If you put down your books
And come outside
For a moment's creole

A horse! an old man! ransom
For a moment's creole
Pass the tequila and damn the socks
For a moment's creole

Now that lad there
Owns a whole corso in Siena,
And my aunt, sweet aunt,
Has a lien on my crown
But they'd all go vagrant
Through the islands of foam
Sweating all the winter
For a moment's creole.

JUBILEE OF EVENING

These are the killers
Linking arms in a circle
Turning in a circle, singing
"We are all killers, hey"
"We are killers all"

Every girl is a cat
Every dog is a boy
Meet me at the reservoir
And I'll hold you blurry
Like a camera in the wind

I wish I was a tentacle
Being ground into paper
I wish you were my leader
Rounding the corner, singing
"Evening, evening"

EASE OF PLAIN

They find it easy enough
To like something or not

To be that animal head still
A bird diving in the throw-in

I get no sense though that
Any word was maybe available

Or the bouncing we walk
Through happily to sit

Except where that is I don't
In the postponed cool to be

In the bother of restaurants
Not to hear, not to listen

DEEP CHERRY

Surgeon dynastic gold point
Windup cattle broadway code
Word lives of the composers
Candlelight doing the pogo
Tipping the stripper love
Your neighbor vinegar French
Fries plastic bag soccer
Yearbook theft grilled
Cappicola perfect
Cholesterol couchette
Fanzine stories by Zelda
Parking indoors washing my
Colors playing with her feet
Cooing and laughing in
Bookstores editing reload
Reviews belief system bonus
Points burnt tongue fuzzy
Headache I want to look at
It I don't want to see you
Gestures of radical affection
Impossible music deep cherry

TALKING TO ANYTHING

I don't even have the coffee
I talk about so much God
Knows how they put up with
Me is a thought how many
People avail themselves of
Bitters come in little phials
Red on the bottom shelf
The angels go roaring down
As when people thinking
Remember they're talking to
You or themselves disguised
As you and they have to in
The French *rendre compte*
Meaning kill the king and
I myself don't mean anything
Under this giant purple sky
That I'd be ashamed to tell
You in our future barn you
Mucking me tending hounds

TEA SLACKS

Tea for the beginnings of
Time well what is that an
Iced coffee I'll have one of
Those never neglect the face of
A person it is information
Itself if the expression is
Wrong but the face beautiful
There is the work you were
Born for if the expression
Fine and the face plain stay
Through the steam if the two
Elements are discomposed
Bless and be friendly but if
The way is fair and the face
What you love congratulation
Is all around you in your
Argument and your repose be
Terrified of crazy people
Keep you two apart and be as
Aroused ensemble as slacks

THE TRUE STORY OF THE APARTMENT

1. THE FRENCH NEW WAVE FILM BY THE POLISH DIRECTOR

Very deep, very sad. They wouldn't allow it in the states.
Dedication. I liked Ram. I went to see Kiss of Death, actually.
And they're both on upper broadway. Who goes to see Rob Roy?
Boys. A hamburger chain making love to what's her name Smart
Babe with red hair. She talks about politics all the time. The
Great liberation guitarists, that's where she got all that crap.
Political or religious—the distinction becomes blurred. In an
Arty way. Speaking about the PLO in favorable terms, Diane Keaton
As Vanessa Redgrave. I'm waiting for that woman to reappear.
He's interrogating us and deciding what we said. He adds his little
Words. Cast doubt? Call today! I have a very passive-agressive
Relationship with circulation directors. *I'm* a circulation director.
He's so our generation, anybody want wine? The Asimov method.
A logical—a short ride from beer to crime. He's not a writer,
He's not a filmmaker, he's not even a softball player.

2. I DON'T KNOW WHAT HIS HISTORY

What did Sam see? He escaped into a church on Twelfth Street.
She has a dog too. Is that really her. It is a way dog. A lint
Brush? You've got a great apartment though. I throw him into the
Tub. We spent about two weeks not being able to sleep. My parents
Had that up when I was a kid. He was fun when I was a kid. He was
A real pain in the butt when I was a kid, he would play Monopoly
With me for real money. Now we get along real well. His life is
About organizing. Cousin Brucie is evil? But if you pet him he's happy.

3. THEY JUST DISGUST YOU—I'M JEALOUS

In the middle of the night does not express joy. I like how much sun they can
Stand, rolling around in the grass making trilling noises.
Being that size and furry. We could wear velvet pantsuits. Do you live
Nearby? No, I work here. As long as we don't get back to John Sayles.
Did you really go to summer camp? Then we ended up gynecology—
Going to college together. That's why this apartment is so expensive.

BOOKS AND THINGS

When I think of Marisa Januzzi
Opening her sixth grade desk
And finding *A Coney Island of the Mind*
My heart is a circular room
Filled with pounding light
And I can smell the tea-scented dust
Up in the back at Books & Things
Where I picked up Ferlinghetti
And a year later Edwin Denby
What a cello of lakes it made me
To meet Marisa outside Kenneth Koch's
Office and to ask her for a poem
For my magazine, undergraduate
Boy! Marisa was working at the St. Moritz
And Kenneth was cranky as Jove
Ferlinghetti was useful to us both,
Marisa, and we were brother and sister
To thousands and thousands who never
Having been to Coney Island and barely
Awake in the first minutes of their mind's day
Pass from the sleep of book reports
To the glorious shifter of poetry

FORCE OF LOCAL PERMISSION

Delay
Gives us a tangible scent
I meet you
And bump
Against you as we walk
Up Union
Square West
You're so
French you think I'm funny
And I'm not
Alone in my
Crumb
Of desire

Other people do their
Other people impressions
You are hoping
Or I am
Something else
Will
Finish our
Beers
Carry us out
But it's work
To speak clearly
About what
Keeps us
The bells are ringing at Grace Church
What time is it?

MEERKAT

In America we are calm.
There is a cat.
The cat may be just outside
Or he may be standing beside our heads
As we sleep. It's cold out.
The cat is loud. We are calm
As thunder, and I'm certain
Of something. It's not on the topic.
Neither is the cobra.
You don't want a cat
You want a meerkat. You don't
Want the
Artists of the Netherlands
To come over
You want a banquet
To be something more than
A big meal eaten by people sitting on benches
You want to shine
A light on the stairs
And see a tiger-headed man smiling climbing
I want to pick you up
And throw you
Into a pile of socks
Ten feet high!

POEM

The ice seller catches the runoff from the elementary school
The elementary school dissolves in the morning cup of coffee
Walking up the street the soapbox derby goes down
As the skirts of long-legged women go up, propelled
By the autumn light breeze, sweater-bringing wind,
And the smell of a particular evening, when she
Dropped by to return the pen she took by accident,
Pausing, mid-sentence, to fix her eye on
The cat playing the floorboards, skidding
Into the future like a drunk pianist…
—*with Elio Schneeman*

TOAST

I'm so happy
Lighting the match to light the oven
To toast the bland bread from the farmer's market
Let me tell you what it was like
Back when I had no toast

I was ashamed to be from an upper middle class family
Every Christmas
I asked for toast
And in the stocking on Christmas morning
Oranges cashews chocolate and toast

I want you to know this about me and toast
I make sandwiches at work
On sliced bread I pop in the toaster
Murry Kaskel the landlord at Teachers & Writers
Brought into the office for his lunchtime cheese and toast

His brother Eddie used to come into my office and say
"Buster, your toast is done"
A couple of hours after the toast was done
I don't usually remember that I've started making toast
I don't have a toaster at home

It's not that I'm poor exactly
I have a great collection of
Library of America and
Pléiade editions
There's just no room in my apartment for a toaster

I miss Eddie
About a month before he died Chris Edgar and I decided

To phone Gary Lenhart up in Vermont
We had Eddie dial him up
"Hello, Gary?" Who's this?" Chris and I howling like dopes

Eddie stopped carrying his gun to the office before I started working there
I don't want to think about my aversion to risk
I want a nice square piece of white toast
Turned over on the aluminum foil in the broiler
And dropped back on to the tiny drops of water

In the hospital or so Ron Padgett told us
Eddie would hoard the cans of Ensure
As he was getting weaker
Eddie had been in the army with his brother
"We sold MacArthur extension cords"

In Ron Padgett's poem about the chocolate milk
And how great it is
The chocolate milk
It seems a little crazy
That a grown man with white hair would be so happy about chocolate milk

Do you know the poem?
Do you know Ron's poem "Birches"
He's responding to Robert Frost's poem about birches
And the mindless poetry of deep significance
As perceived in the symbols of nature

I forget whether it's Ron or Joe Brainard who has a diary from 196something
About dinners of Pepsi and macaroni and cheese
And sometimes when they splurged (Ron and Joe and Pat, Ron's wife)
Dessert of My-T-Fine chocolate pudding
And then there's Alice Notley's journal poems from the seventies

Which in Joel Lewis's social worker description
Are cases of the normalization of poverty
Alice talking about going around to her friends to ask for five dollars
To feed Edmund and Anselm
What do I know I wasn't there

I did see Anselm in the "Waiting on a Friend" video
Allow me to footnote Joel again
Joel used to call up Gary
At around midnight and say "We don't sleep here, we drink coffee"
Here being Joel and Sandy's place

I'm sitting in the kitchen now
Anna's carrying Ponyboy in
She wants to get started with dinner she's offering to cook the steak
I splurged I got paid today
I bought juice, cheese, cereal, beer, dill, sour cream, milk, peas, hash,
    tuna etc.

It's ten-thirty and Anna shouts
Time made Newt Gingrich man of the year?
He has the most major five-o-clock shadow I've seen in my life
I'm a little worn out it's almost Christmas
I live in New York City and its borrowed crap

LET'S FLOAT

We slept in the office
Through loudspeaker
Blasts from the church
O my great mistakes
Because I have changed
The lost world occupies me

Let's float through the city
You know I can't swim
I look for you every morning
Reflecting the flashlight
Eyes of a lost cat—
Claim the free game
The return of the self
Not to glorify those days

TELEKINESIS

Growing up I
Used to think
(Hope?) I could
Change things by
Thinking; picturing
Things as they
Were then
Imagining some
Differences. That's
How it is with you
Sometimes.

MILLION POEMS JOURNAL

What should I say to the Wall Street Journal?

That I meant nothing when I said
I was working on a manuscript of
One million poems? That this was just
Something to say on a calendar by my name,
That it came out of me as I went to press?

Or should I say that since I may
Reasonably wish to live to be 100
And since my twentieth birthday I have
Been writing an average of thirty five poems a day,
Barring some tragedy or catastrophic day
I am scheduled to arrive at poem one million
Circa June 2070?
                        Or that I *must* write
One million poems so that my name, fame
(or vanity and sanity) will not be ridiculous,
And so I've insured my health?

Should I lie? and say it was nothing,
The first million?
That some days I deliberately write
No poems at all,
As a ne'er-do-well dare to the Christmas edifice?

Should I not turn upon it with a yes,
But to admire the thought of quality
Is vulgar and pompous as a lifetime
Passed in the baths of Caracalla?

Or talk Borofsky and his counting,
Or the seconds of my life so far,
That Sappho is a tiny book,
That in her busiest quiet Emily Dickinson finished
Fewer than two poems a day,
That the impossible is corrupt,
It is a basis,
That I feel young, and breathe air
That is certainly new to me,
Though all around people grow tired of it
And say there is no more air;
It is their own lungs, bored of them
But hitched up to talking still,
Like a disused mill,

Not that any poem means a million things
But that anything said truly, known or not known,
That is, a sudden breath
Fills or leaves you,
That's worth seeing
For a second.
There it is—always—in plain sight.

II

No? I'll try again later. (Say that!)
Isn't it funny that the word "million"
Caught them, like a door handle
Or velcro? The Coppertone dog?
And wasn't the Nigerian reporter
Milton Allimadi funny, coming up to me
Before I read to ask would I mind speaking
"About the million poems — my editor is

Very interested." For the crackpot
Of-the-day story, lower left corner
Section Two. "I can't stay
For the reading, there is an African
Film festival at Lincoln Center." Months
Passed. Then, another reading,
No Bar, the same time Ron gives me the job
At Teachers & Writers I didn't get
The year before! He asked such
Questions of me and my father—
In-law to be, and of Kenneth, later on phone.
Poets. Poets? Millions of question marks
My not-yet-23-year-old vibrating corpus
Shaking at the ironic famous thought of not-fame
Not-thought not-even-irony. The story
Came out I bought a dozen copies
They sent one in the mail my dad
Bought a few too, two short poems
Sneaked into print: **THE PARK**
Energetically the straight line of the day
Brings foot after foot of this narrow public land
And **BAD POEM** Put that rock down.
Radio calls come in: a country
Station in Fargo, Michael Feldman's
Wha'D'Ya Know? the Canadian
Broadcasting Corporation.
The Fargo guy really wanted me
To be a crackpot, and the Not Much
Point guy gave up on me after two minutes.
(I developed a taste for the nebbishy
Smelts on that show, but the white jazz
Still gives me the chills.) That was about it
Oh Gillian mentioned the item in her
Gossip column Dirt in the Newsletter

(Which I was editing). Not bad for a
Joke I told Wanda Phipps when she asked
Me how to list my reading with Elaine Randall
At the Poetry Project on Academy Awards night
A night every year when nothing happens no one is even
Killed in New York City which is therefore murder
For people who edit events listings in free papers
As my what? Colleague? Classmate? Neil Strauss
Did at that point for the Marithe Francois Girbaud
Ad in the Voice that went something like
Jordan Davis is reading from his
Collection of a million poems
Which is about as many oscars as
Clint Eastwood is going to win tonight.
(Unforgiven.) Anyway. Where are the
Million poems now, you may ask, shouldn't
I be going on 115,000 as it gets to be
2002? Er, I'm behind. But I'm pleased to see
It's only 95 percent off track and not 99.9 as
I think I may have stated in a fit of anger
Sometime in 1996. Please forgive those old
Moods of mine, I'm trying to be more
Available to all my affect now and therefore
Less spooky, tonally. They say anger
Is necessary, or useful, for getting things done,
But I prefer to think all you need is a goal.

READY DESIRE

Ready to feel
              I called you

I wanted to carry you
Through the maze of lights
Lacking imagination
Wire of wife
              Passion is
Not something like booze
You have its rust upon you
On the axle on the airwave
To desire to desire
                    What
Could be more calming
                          But then

What exactly is wrong
With what anyone feels
As though the real truth
Asks me something
                    I don't
Know

COPPER BEECH

The plaster needs fixing
And the grout in the tub is gray
The plants are back from brown
The cheap rose in its third bloom
Dianthus blossoms cluster at a stem
Like geraniums
                    a feather driven
Out through the comforter cover
For the cold summer breeze

Confused the feather goes out
Over the empty double candlestick
And the trees are full of light seeds
Someone with a young voice is calling
Someone it's after eleven-thirty.
The dark hair of women in films
And the brown curly hair it's not red.

The police stand fat on Second Avenue
Tic-tac-toe drawn on my heart
Every autumn to ask the question
Of the red-blue air at quarter-turns,
What question? what question?
A purple cardinal whistles it
To a white chickadee.
The geese in the sky are black
Flying off in different directions,
Branches of a copper beech.

LAND CAMERA

After
The self-regarding religiosity
Of music-critics shuts itself
Lilting in a mirrored box
If I thought anything was endless
                               and the cloud
A fixture, as breathing twenty dollars
Meet and hold ourselves aloft
On a fine breeze, a jet
Distraction we agree on but if
The intellectual future depends
On essays
                        below this line we are
Having a parallel experience again
An evening of stars and kids
A pasty and probably anti-semitic vocabulary
Impatience having led in this case to
A desk in a Euclid, IL
Office where no one anticipates
The onslaught of radical decency
But they're happy to join when it comes

HAIKU

The dog stands by the window
Barking endlessly—
We are playing baseball.

Nobody in the tollbooth,
Nobody at the snackbar
We are not talking.

SOME EFFECTS OF THE BOOK

I am shared by ivy
Which is going down to the tuning forks
Of salty river. The pencils are stacked in the brickyard
And the rented barrels commence
Their collisions. It is a scientific certainty
That the most beautiful women in New York come from Irvington,
New York. My wife is in Massachusetts.
Peerless and radiant.
I thought those words on line
And I think the words "compass", "rations", "lumber",
Caffeine and theophylline have tomorrow
Which is a sexy deterioration of these promises
Memorable speech my ass! Haverstraw gloats in the distance.

NOTEBOOK AND CHOIR

Sojourning in the particular Brechtian nonsense offered
By the supermarket intercom—a song Sting sang
"Attention shoppers"—then back to the vibraphone
Put on the red light. I don't own any railroads
Anymore, but I love the tiny choir that sings as the 4:20
Local gets in and the mommy waves both hands
It's a couple of sustained notes
Faster than the notebook wants me to know.

REGULAR DIAMONDS

Come on for blue shadows
In the environmentally frequent crawdad
Ur fazed, flue of which the arch crack'd
Improvisation stet. For as it is blue
Sounds on the mart, you are my garden decisive.
True now and accidental, I am calm enough to prop you up
And know you like you lead me to believe you like.
Laughter in the water trees dark. Come on for blue shadows.

SOMEONE ON THE CARPET

He, seeking his hello,
Hears the brooding of gold coupons,
His bed against the window.

He begins his first census:
"When I refused to describe heaven"
"I was sitting on a giant's nose."

He hears the coupons unlace sails,
Cement negatives of their faces,
A little apple in a broken vat.
Four orange flags over an oval in the street.

"In winter stomp puddles,"
"Go out and slip."
"Invent a new crime,"
"Outline power."

A bright pink tongue
And soaping down the street
Mimic formally
His experience of sugar—

"Here is then what that art will be:"
"Pictures of exception,"
"Deceptive continuity."

An anchor on a mountain of tires.

POEM MIDDLE OF THE NIGHT

When I wake up in the morning or the early afternoon
And the meaning which was formerly if not connected to
Then associated with the streets and open sky has gelled
Into the kind of translucent paste atop slices of cake
In a chinese bakery, the kind selling Ovaltine and Horlick's
By the cup, and words having been left to take care
Of the growth of the spirit and understanding have not
Known what was meant by the assignment but have done
What I see now, waking, propped on an elbow, noise
Of helicopters just outside, as a reasonable enough job

The woman in bed next to me sitting up laughing at
Northanger Abbey and my mood is irrigated,
I carry the cat down the alphabet and he resists
And wake up to white rhomboids among the cable
Every package wondering whether to be or not
Ripped open and consumed, dispatched love letters
Trembling on the watery surface of unused time
The declined languages spread into like oil. Midnight
Times noon, in story-language, which is the eventual
Homeland, math, and release from suffering

SONNET

The perfection of the science-fiction novel is the end of love
        as we've known it.
Walking down the narrow streets, eyes meet someone with larger eyes.
It must be an Anglican service. Take this ring,
The size of the largest eye I have ever seen.
It was part of a scene that was also occupied by an immense detailed
        beautiful red blue yellow green and white landscape painting
           including figures of the Holy Virgin her son and their admirers
              by Pinturrichio in Spello in 1563.
The burgeoning mystery of wedlock is not lost.
It is simply that I walk down this street.
My permanent affection, which is not all my feeling, is for you.
I was born to everyone. This doesn't mean I am free.
Words attack me. They attract me, which is the same thing
If you're a target.
I won't be here forever.
When the bridge is raised, a crowd gathers, waiting for it to go down.

The periodicity of blue is the letter G.
Why have I picked this letter? You answer me. Why shouldn't we refuse
To mystify each other? For, life is simple:
To iron one shirt, to make up a bed.
The day I gave up falling in love for you, all-out running the beach.

ARE YOU TO BE MY NAMIBIA?

                                         Or
Therapeutic spaceship tantrums getting it

On with the suspicion of music as allergy,
As stuff in code looks like a nutter did it.
This all you could drag over the keyboard

And your racetrack of slowness would pop up
In the air like an electrical being,
One not so bent-down as to bedouin a library

But give me your gravity—I want to make
New hours with it, I want its finish.

ROTTEN FLOOR

The tiles on the floor were jostled
Apart and the plywood underneath
Was showing so I decided to take
It up. Hammer and prybar and up
And lo below the toilet the boards
Were rotted clean away.
      "Ohhhh..."
I said, broke as can be, to the earth
In the basement below.
      "Yup,"
Said the earth, "I was waiting
For someone to notice that. And while
You're here, thanks for the compost."
"You're welcome," I thought, pleased.
The earth was quiet.
It was depressing and cold in the
Smoky bathroom. "Oh no!" Anna
Said, leaning in over my shoulder.
"The floor is totally gone!"
      "It's
Not so bad," I said, applying
A hanky to the boards. "It
Looks better than it did with the tile"
"Ah that's just like you" someone said
I couldn't tell, I was thinking
About Africa, monetary policy, and
My poetry.

THE PARADE OF THE NOTEBOOKS

As the train
Elbows and shrugs
Around Spuyten Duyvil
And French women
Run down the aisle
Looking for window seats
To stare at the river
At eleven p.m.
The notebooks file by

The black
Artist's journal
A plank of wrinkles
It opens to show us
Translations from the French
Of Pierre Reverdy
Part of every poem
Of his collected works
Is here—hundreds
Of sturdy bright pages
The translator has been shy
Getting a couple of words
Here and there

And here in black canvas
Called subway journal
Sunset journal
Coffee journal—fake names!
It is only
Descriptions of people

The author has fallen
In love with
For a few minutes
An hour at most
Look! the notebooks
With shields on the covers
Are coming! In the front
In blue oh the pages
Are watermarked
Deep pale yellow
Ink of fountain pens
For prose-in-poems
The gentle bastard!

That blare of black
The composition marble
Covered notebook
Of different kinds of time
Laundry time happy hour
Half time anticipatory
Consciousness lilac time
The egret in the arm
Two o'clock eastern
BBC time school time
Asleep in the park

The dark flower book
Collaborations with the self
Jungles of chrome
Patriarchs in drag
Mice running
Along the moulding

Ah in this canvas-
Covered book words turn
Into stories an egg
Becomes the barn the
Typewriter under the helmet
Looks out on evenings
At antique light
Etymologically twitching
The darning put aside
The covers pulled back

The coloring book
Of the conference of the birds
The hoopoe's beak is open
And he is calling
The air swirls around him
The trees and bicycles of the desert
Swirl around him

The gold cork-covered book of
The valley of naked strangers at night
Look down into the valley
As the ocean comes into it
And the people shine in the moonlight
On the rocks and on the grass
They are standing still
And moving out into the water
As they push in the water
The water lights up around them

The mirror-covered
Notebook for describing skaters—
"The crowd goes by so quickly
And smoothly

That a heavy young man
His cap on backwards
And smoke streaming from his nose
Looks down and without knowing why
Begins to cry"

The art-averaging notebook with
La Grande Odalisque on the front
And the Breakfast Room
On the back starts with
The room of liminal color
Shimmering in
As you flip the pages
Poised and resplendent
The grande odalisque
In optical pantaloons
And white pendant breasts
She sits deeply in sight
As the purple orange and green
Hammer flat the air the walls
And the jungle outside
Replacing by the end
The curtains and the
Chaise longue

The notebook of tire rubber
And reflectors
Unpatented objects
The movie tarpaulin
Twenty meters across
And catching the movies

The lab book
For the pasteurization
Of crossword poems
And their carbons
Quadrilateral as sound

The math book of
A fat man
In a math uniform

The most advanced quality
Gives best writing features
& gives satisfaction to you

The anonymous
And unfinished
Novel notebooks
Strew possible
Worlds from their
Hats as they
Somersault and
Crumple themselves

At last we are tired of this mood and cyan
Collapse the spyglass
Undo the wing nuts from the stilts
And catch cab homebound before the fogs rise

WOMAN (A.S.)

The red moon is a banjo
A jinx is a flat rate
I am a dropshot
Arizona is the sunrise of a fuckoff
Tonight is the uncompiled code of an iced coffee
A dart is the jimmy of a limousine
My homeland is the dogma of brimming
Turpentine is the Paul McCartney of your letting me know
My lever is tomorrow
A starling is a skinny boy
A drifter is a paragraph
Dehydration was your joyride
Pacman is a percentage
Spelling is diamonds
The grey grass is a conformist
Her hat is Alaska
Her smile is a plastic mouse
Adios is her dreadlock
High-five is the rated G of a shopping cart boutique
The pervert is a vaccination of centipedes
An armband is the fossil of a poetry bookie
Glasses are the booklet of toast
Marina is the destruction of copper
A box of nursery school paintings is a tree in the shade
An alarm clock is a fire at sea
A plaid jacket on a dog is the weather underground
Being tired on Friday is the Colorado River
The dharma of sunshine is egg cartons
The pope of gunmetal is a fine wine
The bad teeth of the cricket wicket are blue and white china
A gold box on the dresser is a photograph of sleep

My time with you is a cast-iron bank
I'm Mother Superior thrown in the snow
I'm the headlights of a car at twilight
I'm my own spoiled son
I'm a shop window of things for you
I'm a boy meant to be a girl
I'm a killer of eagles
I'm a blues singer in Calgary
I'm Jesus riding with the cavalry
I'm naked in my fur
I'm your birthday
I'm a round the world train
I'm the moment of death
I'm the cow-reporter at the bar
I'm the 100-yard dash
I'm a baseball in heaven
I'm a tight tank top
I'm a vamping twin
I'm a tractor trailer in midtown
I'm one red light on in the building
The west wind is a black lion of linen
Blurry electricity is the handprint of graham crackers
A window is the bigamist of curving
A coffee can is the geranium of afros
A quarrel of carnivals is a fox of Coca Cola
A crown of wallets is a shipwreck of parking lots
A fool of smudges
A liar of straight lines
I am the snow of an Irish girl entraining
For the sun of a ticket is the plain face of math
Someone is shouting
Someone is smoking on the platform
Someone is nodding her head with her glasses and headphones
        on and looking down

Nodding over and over
That concrete on the edge of the tracks next to a fence looking over
    a street and some factory lots
That looking and analyzing and thinking and bossing are primary
But not like swimming
The fear of neighborhoods
The theory of bonus points
So-proud being listens to people look and talk
There's the city now
The business page

THOSE KEROUACS MAY YET BE SUNS RA

A preset forest—

If the page is mainly blank,
are we not to write on it

must the future always be so schizophrenic—

is it less than a month? a room is blank
will remain consistent only when
there is a wide variety of situations?

the multiple face of a napoleon wave—
granny stars in silhouette—
a dollar's weather glitter monkey—
coal the saxophone wings of chaos—

possibility (or too much make up)?

overlays to an older pagan work—

asynchronous—
is content a means to synchronization—

depth meaning what, opacity?

before all else fails—
how the liar misses harmony—

experiments in consensus—

to be graceful opposes a general synchronization—

why I don't want my reading enhanced—

a very engine against the unknown, to be dignified—

EPISTEMOLOGY WANTS YOU

Across town—town, with you every day
To ejudicate the boundaries I carry the bones
Out of town—chuck the junk—free the slaves—
Up and down again too soon—free the slaves
From their slaves—free again in the street
Shadows buoying on the bow rewinding and then
In this each as important as the other system
Nothing isn't singular—back up coughing and looking

Scrimmage line of cab doors the Airborne Express
Lady with the jheri curl is home. Gruppo Decalogo
On 22nd Street, walks by nodding to Steely Dan
It's more like the soviet or radiation or poor nutrition
As I prop my sweatered elbow on TV. General Delivery.
Dragonfly first thing—the transmission
Of unknowing isn't God to football and chess—
View of things as opposed coming from a church
On the stone wall by the piled-up slovenly sod
Believe more or less except the track meet quiz show

The only thing today is good that runs where you go
To write your love notes in superlative common
Calling fighting condensing each shorter than the last
The song is a uniform to wear when you slow down and they go by
What can't be done wide and with their hair up
In the crisp blue coat little movies and TVs
Wider than sunset bluer than life the going treelight in a storm shop
On somehow life-giving carpets do you take pleasure in the way people
    bounce along
Enclosed in linen feel a surprising give

Archival looks and rhyming walks she's carrying herself with her teeth
Sweetness of a clean nursery a building so tagged it's it
Being good meaning paying the bills in battle
And thunderstorms and what for familiar procedure
You do believe in control or no the diagonal school
Negotiating visiting rights with the sun portfolio dangled
To the bottom half of walks flips its racket walking
The half songs dispense with us then someone
Girl looks down so far says hi! And it's over

The way the grass grows let the cane fall
Motherhood and food to the wandering eye
The need for screenplays light from a basement apartment
The cough is catching they thought epics were handbooks
Owner and dog march with soda though they didn't think of it
If the cab on the cobbles makes a strike did the Ancient Greeks have fun
The whistle of a plane at the earth making up for all the dull stories
In the sunny church darkness the toppling inevitable newsclip
Up to the top of the grass enclosures the dust of the moon on you

Short gloom plashes dote and raid the siren'd pickup
I don't answer to you I look at people at angles
In windows fire drawl the time limit but barely
Closeout meetings below make a protest movie
Block parade kisses upright a fallow melisma shade
The one of us shore questions on the piling mitigation croupier
Lifelike accessories proposed battening sundress mosaic
The cruel moods out of me as well as you wear your pants
That is warmth and divestment told cat-style without regard
For which I make labials strewing the tools, spooking
The sky rake, hatdance carhorn degree, elevated crooks

Yes is a curse to them a skateboard on a guard rail
Crows can't get to, time the university of no
And of duplication shadow on a screendoor, a doorbell
Birdsong nothing distance crows can't get to, time
Is time to blank and repeat that when it's answered
It comes unspooled as soon as the prude does the damage
The beginning of rhyme—time for a spanking

Man behind me keeps rasping all right then all right them
The wrist shakes as the fuselage of the head car shakes
They twine their flight paths my parents cut out articles
To rattle me, for instance red-head finches I don't need
This one about tenants rights valium only to keep the head
Frugal with chirrups fibrillates the cherry tree—mosquito
Families count, look out is a sewing hand in flight,
A finch is the fall of train river slush organizations

Isn't what's
To get through
Illustrating to you what goes different
On the avenue rises and all the fiancées cheer a student
Settlement—they had no switch rail shining—
Is doing but they know well take birth control
Use both sides if necessary.) Since his murder in 1995

Argument dogood carbondate Buster Brown
Barefoot and pragmatic
Hungry angry lonely tired some functions of memory
Elapse and coordinate known as playing the changes
The way etymology has taken over me
Searching for bad blocks and not to sacralize
Could be organized hallway cardamom
They read energy crisis for lunch

Actuary pinnacle chute colossus
Firewall residue plain as the rinse
On the rivets crossing the jack

Globular booming gratuitous show-off flirt
They're repelled by arborvitae likewise ficus butterfly
Goodbye renegade traders
Speeding arbiters of sunset Trixie
Command the highwind sapphires

Tablecloth flip like a skirt chair partly in shade
To do your job keeps you the matter rests
Escapes   it's not laziness

O BOTH

If I carried you all that way
Upside darling would we be less
Convinced the future is out to lose
The evidence we meant to conceal

And the path in the dark looking
Valiant (page-boy bob) well to movies
Let's go unsupportably to push and be
Judged and jaded and smudged and say

Boo the second we see what sleep
We've stored in the account and what
Hours and days we'll manage to bequeathe
The fast-drying klezmer tsking our deal

Time was we were O you star
An item tallied   skinny glitter

TO THE ZEE AND BACK

Givingthestrengthofremoteness

                Ta   a   v
    Above   suave   ivy   coves
    And requiring
               Everything   sing again
Sing and jog past neoexhibitionists
      nervous and cold
                        ah   life wires tile and pine
Exaggerated sleep of stuck-to-window-door

                     Posters bowed
A statistical sample of eye-level
My time with you   SEA
                                  LEVEL

                                    rocks

   *

The carving board

   |
   V

Right over the grass   Climate patrol

(Standing on the ledge to smoke)   You
                                           Have
                                           To
                                           Go
                                           Where
                                           It's
                                           At

SQUIB   VENISON   the
                      RACK   true mulch
                                    of the
                                    dictionary

  To do some good
        luck!

     Blank pout

of a governness (sp?)

       quilted landscape   e.g. coleus hillside
       and the sheer   reprimand of it

       the oat   a goat ate

     vibe-copper, life thief!

     They were secret together
         running and smoking
              a cigar
                    on New
                    Year's eve
                    and after

   *

And then they were low-level operatives

looking for mass destruction

                              a miss of
                              pinball

                              a mess of midsections
                              taro rations

                                        Betsy Beep

                              Purim two by two

                              Still stuck depicting life on earth
                              Some urgings
THE TRUTH   Chess move

We painted the paper with glue   Rictus   baby summer   chiasmus
scattered glitter o'er the surface

                                        know-nothing
Arts and Crafts was a vital movement
in 19th century American design   After lunch man is fat
                              In the book of love Hazlitt
I am not going to   disguises himself as a rosy charwoman   fights crime!
literary conventions
                    The books we read are the books we don't write
What would happen to me if I had thoughts   I am storms
Before words. Why don't those bugs   The sort of
                                             information I want is

Come back here?   I don't

                    Lovely diagonal

        *

So   the   time   we   pass

taxes   shine

         and   shore

The   style   of   clothing
The   song   in   the   air

Some   glee

    *

The maths
Were under   blemi
                 schwa   glimmer

    time   and   words

Count your shadows

Apples light a block

mountain zee the mud up to me
Any   name   riots

The   mom   is
What   augmented
                        I am absolute sigh
Analyze my fat
Our custom—take love when you get it

The screws from the exist sign
Easter Island   no snow

        no   n

   *

Go on
Important
Thimble   baby

The conversation bears into the moon's trace

You're dogging me
Too groomed

Wet bicycles in the grass

      Penny   —>   bless you!

A horse carries the land aside
                all my shores of shots-on-goal
Protect downtown
                    closer to chanting
go giraffes go!

Where the runners go
and the smell of a paint store,
                    plastic and sweet
      I like how you don't
particularly want to be liked

   *

Shrugs slurry   the love
so incidental it   laps   the quavering
derivable fatherhoods

light from the street
quickly   the tropical storm is quarrying me

In the evening the air time
Is what we have for all in all,
Indexed by quantity, amalgamated,
As I might map a piano room
Or skim the concordances
In the evening, a fan of modes.

This system, or view if you prefer,
Has a soothing remedy for trumps
And other clevernesses, acknowledging
The alphabet, the structure,
Coordinating maddening redundancies
And dispelling them. One trope one vote.

The possibility of plurality, however—
A smile gone cold on the words
"No confidence"—does not the need
To know what next manufacture
The filament syntax? Huh? Gimme five.
Hear thoughts, static, and laugh.

EXPLODED VIEW

High molarity of huns at this reading
Envisioning projects in terms of the supplies social terse
Farmers at the pharmacy that was restoring
Local dubiety what responsibility were you thinking of
Blink some
Architecture door opens a flea under the microscope black and tan
Coast guard didn't mean it partly cloudy, party loudly
Clues to the language crude came flaring *the moon slowed everybody down*
Codex moment bloop single multiple Kansans hush reply quietly eluding
Who was at the ball? Did we take the quiet over the bar foment descant
Cloisonne rode over on my swivel chair
Darkly preaching there's a wet one didn't the ease conceal me
You're not alone ball point poem
Orders for durable goods blow me up trapped rapidity what can you approximate
Chamois cloth fool fume
Whose ether trapeze as they asked it
How is your Maverick problem kazoo interns of posse
Tanks are rubbery who's divorcing me now
More than twice proof is in the poontang why not loaf more by which I mean
    do I remember
Each day he would trowel
Who's absent now
Have we melded? Transactions are jaded tigers hate amulets? Mandates go on
Carom all you want vote softly
Charismatically pendulum tea soaked
Chaos isn't disrepair
Maybe too retro who's the sophist front magician ornery a pocket full
Economists had forecast plumes of time keys jingling blue season
Some sacking xeroxed phrases rotate the fires
Please don't tell God the rivers receded
Roost shuttle home Monday goon keno

Go on, get grotesque retreat
When I met you I was coated reprogram
Each day the world travels clothed choruses where does it tingle

LAST MUCHAS GRACIAS

Why anything gets
to anybody—

she's beautiful,
she's happy,
something's burning—

so you find
hesitation attractive—

so you give creedence
to movies and songs—

Animal prints are
automatically excellent—

Use is quantifiable—

At least lens is fourth
of its functions—

What do you mean
do I come here often—

Are sovereignty
and independence
outdated, both?—

Enough haiku life,
I want kids—

Overhearing has a time
and a place—

The heft of fifteen
minutes—

I'm only sleeping—

The sexiness of
cleaning your teeth
with your tongue—

Are we best friends, then—

I like how you encroach—

Service like independence
is relative—

A future of cash—

Cash is a drug—

Driving is a drug—

Drugs are blimps—

Are you really on PCP?—

Do you have to be in
public to have a
decent conversation
with yourself—

How many Sundays
can you work on
mailing lists—

Are priests what marriage
is for, then—

One version or
another will do,
as will beauty alone—

Did he say virgin—

Is that the real
Miss America over there—

She's cringing and
preexisting—

Intelligence is heavy—

In vivo is a nice way
of saying "live"—

What is a flea?—

Applause, christmas
glass, flash cut—

Which scam is this—

A road without a map—

Some more flashes
and a dog waits
to be served—

I'll take monarchy—

400 monarchs—

The social stratificaton
in that room—

But if there were
a bar for kings
and queens—

All bars are such—

What errands did
you have to keep
you so long from
this lap—

NASHVILLE

Hegemonic rooty-toots placate

                Gethsemane collocations punk rock

Go one at a time
auto bodies dispatched to marshes

Flood the bog

                              and smile,

                you're saying hi

But thinking about how to escape false futures

So volunteer some true one

And without barf tango, if you please

Do not volunteer us for death postcards
Profound as our habiliments be
O stalwarts of sodfarm irrigation
I myself cuddling with fir trees' shadows

                            NOT REAL

          meaning unavailable for comment

look! An apiary

a blue glint in the woods

        the woman in front saying 'Jesus'
        every twenty seconds

I bequeath quangos to Holy Goose

EXTRA GRIDS BEMOAN VEHICULAR CUTBACKS

        a gloss

Freedom is apprehended in a belief.
Standards of obsequiousness ensue.
Signage corroding packets, blood school tips.
A song reveals general darkness.
The plaza is overrun by escape.
A shack is voted and unvoted.
The recourse button sticks and fame leaks into the atmosphere of delay.
A pair of children play music outdoors.
Long neutral, the quiet becomes charged.
Someone peels an orange.
The anonymous market opens for the evening.

BRA MAKES CHALLENGE TO OUIJA GROUP

They picked me right up off the boat
Set me on a flatbed
Fastened me into my opalescent pinions
And graduated me with a champale across my ass

Unfurnished rooms don't impregnate salt lack
But the France apparent preys on their tines

      Victory light is deregulated
   So's sex pez

SAME THE PIRATE

I'd like to be a calligraphic homestead for vertigo
Bemoaning overpleasure   bismillah!   I would

Glitter turquoise skull graffit   giraffe pomp

    As though meditation were easy

Things to do in Abidjah

     Eat chocolate

  Pull

    gently!

Participate in wholesale banditry

  Change your mask

          say hi!

Protozoa attached firmly to shiny propulsion
     Glistening and purple and you strain

   A trout!

Laborers rearrange the medium-sized stones
And descend by the glowing pylon marked

       W
       A
       T
       C
       H

       Y
       O
       U
       R

       S
       T
       E
       P

To a varnished

                encrusted with macadam

                                access road

(She levels me with a teaspoon)

                (Shofar love note barricado)

increases oil viscosity
destroys your car!   Gosub primadonna
raids on the cake

Tipping one of the logs on its side with the end of a new log
I uncover the char.
The new log goes in and in a second the stove is hissing.
Fire lights from the back forward.
Smoke and vapor rush back through the stove,
The old log rippling with white orange and blue flames,
Gold-red coals falling forward into the collapsing drifts
Of ash at the side.
Then sirens and whistles, a radio near a station
As the bark, flames combed back
As if it were hurtling forward,
Bends up away from the log.
The flue is as loud as someone walking in another room,
occasionally pressing the side of her beer can.
I cross my legs the other way.
Now it sounds like a chickadee.

It made my mom
        totally
get an electric guitar

my sister owns that boa

I'm a dolphin, smart!
(But she can't hyphenate
for *anything*)